It's Not Your Fault!
You Have Dirty DNA

Edie Bayer

Glorified Publishing

PO Box 8004

The Woodlands TX 77387

ISBN: 1-946106-46-1

ISBN-13: 978-1-946106-46-9

DEDICATION

Dedicated to Cherise and Bobb – Forever Mine.
Know I love you! There has never been a moment when you were unloved.
Even as you were sinning, I still loved you, and I ever shall.
You are mine. You are branded.
You are my child and I will NEVER change my mind about you.
Love, God

It's Not Your Fault! You Have DIRTY DNA!

CONTENTS

ACKNOWLEDGMENTS

It's all God. Thank you Jesus!

Edie Bayer

CHAPTER ONE: DIRTY DNA

Jesus set me free today! I am free from the bondage of guilt and remorse, and He wants YOU to be, too!

I want to say to those people, especially parents, who are carrying guilt or remorse for something that you have done, something done to you, or something that has happened as a result of your actions: DON'T!

We should not carry guilt and remorse, especially where our children are concerned, and this is why:

You probably were operating under a curse – what I will refer to as "DIRTY DNA". This means you were not truly liable!

Honestly, you may still be operating under this curse and have "Dirty DNA", but thankfully, there is an easy fix! Now, I am not saying that you have an exit ramp here, and you should not shoulder any blame or endure the repercussions. But I would like to share with you what the Lord shared with me, to enable me to walk in freedom and uprightly before Him...and not be dragging around shame, disgust, guilt and regret wherever I go!

Wouldn't you like to be free from all that? God wants that, too!

Okay! Let's go!

CHAPTER TWO: HOW DID THIS HAPPEN?

Let's say that you had parents who were unsaved, or like me, were saved when you were a little older. I was almost in my twenties when my folks gave their lives to the Lord. So, before being saved, your parents, like mine, probably did things against God's statutes.

I am sure that they broke at least one (or more) of the ten commandments, potentially even after they were saved. Now, even if they didn't, someone before them in their ancestral bloodline probably did. Honestly, who knows WHAT our ancestors were doing a couple hundred years ago before the internet and cable television, right?

> *"The fathers shall not be put to death for [the sins of] their children, nor shall the children be put to death for their fathers; [only] for his own sin shall anyone be put to death,"* (Deuteronomy 24:16).

According to Deuteronomy and other places, every man must die for his own sin. This is pretty good news, actually! You can die a physical death because of what you do, but you can also die a spiritual death on your own, too! However, the opposite is also true – we cannot ride our parents' coattails into heaven. But, I digress.

Don't get hung up on the negatives here! This is just background to build a case. There is an incredibly easy way to fix this! Keep reading.

Even though each has to die for their own sins, there is a fate that is sometimes worse than death – that of watching our children coming into harm's way. This happens by "GENERATIONAL CURSES."

"The offspring of Israel ... stood and confessed their sins and the iniquities of their fathers," (Nehemiah 9:2).

CHAPTER THREE: GENERATIONAL CURSES

*"The LORD is slow to anger, and abundant in lovingkindness, forgiving wickedness and transgression; but He will by no means clear the guilty, visiting (avenging) the wickedness and guilt of the fathers on the children, to the third and **fourth generations** [that is, calling the children to account for the sins of their fathers],"* (Numbers 14:18 AMPC).

Without repentance, generational curses go into effect immediately upon sinning and are passed on from generation to generation – up to the fourth generation. Simply because a generation was cursed would cause it to sin, creating a downward spiral.

Anyone who sinned during the years of the curse would extend the duration of the curse for many, many years...right down to this generation. In addition to that, each generation that sinned would add their curse to the existing curse/s that were already on the next generation. This would compound the curses exponentially for each subsequent generation born under a curse.

Although I don't have a scripture for it, the sins committed would also probably increase in evil with each passing generation. That would be because people tend to become conditioned to the atmosphere around them and accept it as "normal". This would be why the Bible says people will call evil good and good evil, become lovers of self and eventually completely deny Christ...because of complacency toward sin, because it's "normal" behavior. Sounds like today!

> *"Woe to those who call evil good and good evil, who put darkness for light and light for darkness, who put bitter for sweet and sweet for bitter!"* (Isaiah 5:20 AMPC).

These generational curses in our family lines are still in effect today, even though it may have been over a hundred years ago, or even longer, since the sin occurred. The Bible assumes a generation is forty years, so it could be as long ago as one hundred twenty to one hundred sixty years since the sin was committed...and we are still paying for it!

CHAPTER FOUR:
THERE IS A SUPERNATURAL FIX!

But don't stop reading yet! Here comes the fix! Since your parents or someone else in your bloodline did something against God, even unwittingly or in total ignorance, there is still a penalty that must be paid. That is, after all, why Jesus went to the cross for us, to pay for our sin in our place.

So, watch this: Your parents, who sinned and never repented of it, have now activated a generational curse that falls on you.

WHAT? I know, it's grossly unfair because you didn't even do anything wrong, yet you still got a curse on your life, from your own parents, or maybe theirs or maybe your great-grandparents. But, those are the rules of engagement for being a Christian – we live a supernatural life. Thankfully there is a supernatural remedy, as well!

By the way, to do away with the argument that Jesus cancelled out all generational curses when he died,

7

Jesus said he didn't come to do away with the law, but to fulfill it. Look here:

> "Do not think that I came to do away with or undo the [a]Law [of Moses] or the [writings of the] Prophets; I did not come to destroy but to fulfill. **18** For I assure you and most solemnly say to you, until heaven and earth pass away, not the smallest letter or stroke [of the pen] will pass from the Law until all things [which it foreshadows] are accomplished. **19** So whoever breaks one of the least [important] of these commandments, and teaches others to do the same, will be called least[important] in the kingdom of heaven; but whoever practices and teaches them, he will be called great in the kingdom of heaven," (Matthew 5:17-19 AMP).

The truth is that even though Jesus DID come to do away with generational curses – along with sickness, disease, poverty, and eternal death in hell – those blessings are NOT automatic! The blessings for which Jesus died to give us MUST be activated by us.

Want proof? Ok. Have you ever said, "The Sinner's Prayer"? YOU must ask for salvation. It's not automatic, otherwise, every person on earth would be automatically saved. That would be "Game Over" for the devil! But that is NOT the way it is.

Salvation is a free gift, right? Absolutely. But you must still activate it by faith, confess and believe in your heart.

> "...because if **you** acknowledge and confess
> with your mouth that Jesus is Lord
> [recognizing His power, authority, and majesty
> as God], and believe in your heart that God
> raised Him from the dead, you will be
> saved," (Romans 10:9 AMP).

It is the same with ALL the gifts and blessings of God. One must confess, believe in your heart and activate it by faith. Oh, and one more thing – you must BELIEVE that you RECEIVE.

"If they confess their iniquity, and the iniquity of their fathers, with their treachery that they committed against Me ... then will I remember My covenant," (Leviticus 26:40, 42).

CHAPTER FIVE: IT'S NOT YOUR FAULT

Now, back to the beginning. If you did something sinful when you were younger, such as fornication, adultery, drugs, alcoholism, or worse – and you are carrying guilt and/or remorse – DON'T. Chances are very good that your DNA was stained by something that your parents, your grandparents, or maybe your great-grandparents did, which opened a door into the demonic realm, manifesting in the evil, wicked, sinful thing that you did (or are doing).

Did you see that? It's not your fault. It was the curse, and you were acting under it. Yes, you were physically present; you participated, and may even have made the decision, or so it would seem. But the curse is the thing that opened the door for it to present itself to you.

Listen, in my family, my mother is Scottish. Masonry, the precursor to satanism, is rampant in Europe, particularly in Scotland. When I asked my Mom if there was any history of Masonry in our family line, she said, "Och, aye, hen!" (Translated, this means, "Oh, YES, daughter!")

I was so completely shocked! I asked her if she and my Dad had done anything to cleanse our family bloodline and she said yes. I was relieved at that moment. It took me several years before I realized the ramifications of this huge smear on our family's bloodline: our DNA was Dirty.

You MUST see this picture and apply it to your own life!

Here is why: She and my Dad didn't get saved until I was 18. They would not do something spiritually mature like what we are talking about today, the cleansing of generational bloodlines, until much later in their Christian walk. I didn't learn about it until I was in my forties, so they probably were saved for years before they did it.

That means that I was in my mid-to-late twenties, or potentially older, before they cleansed their DNA, effectively removing the curse from their family line for Masonry up through their lives... but not beyond.

CHAPTER SIX: BORN UNDER A CURSE

Hear me: They cleansed the family bloodlines from THEM back through time, so the generational curses that were in effect on *their lives* up until that moment went away.

However, this did nothing for my life, or my children's lives because we were already under the curse before they did this. Had they done it before I was born it would have impacted my life and my children's; but since I was born under a curse, grew up and later became accountable for my own actions, I would have to cleanse my own generational bloodlines myself. My children, who are grown, will have to do it for themselves, too.

But by my twenties, because I was born under a curse from my parents, grandparents and other ancestors, I had already done a LOT of stuff against God. I broke many of the commandments as well as the laws of Moses, simply because I didn't know them, nor did I care! Regardless, ignorance is no excuse in the eyes of the law in the United States, and it isn't in the Kingdom, either. My infractions invoked even more generational curses onto my unborn children, grandchildren and all future descendant's to be born to my family line.

But guess what? I had a daughter before I was 20. She was born under a curse, too. So now My daughter is walking under those same curses in her life, those activated by my parents or some other predecessor in her and my bloodline – plus whatever curses were dropped on her by my sinful behavior, plus her own. They have just been heaped on her, exponentially!

"We acknowledge, O Lord, our wickedness and the iniquity of our fathers, for we have sinned against You," (Jeremiah 14:20).

CHAPTER SEVEN: REPENTENCE IS THE KEY

SO – How DO we get rid of generational curses and the accompanying sinful behavior to keep it from coming back? How do we get rid of that sin that stained our parents, who passed that stained DNA down to us?

Well, part of it is already outlined above – Activate by Faith, Confess, Believe, Receive.

Now, here is where it gets hard, and easy at the same time. Even though I can rid my own bloodline of generational curses going forward, she must do it for herself. That is the easy part. The hard part is that she must do it for herself!

This means that my daughter (*insert your daughter, son, sister, cousin, husband or other*) must recognize that it is a generational curse that is at work in her life by understanding that all of our actions have spiritual sources and spiritual ramifications.

FINALLY! HOW TO DO IT! How does my daughter

get rid of a curse that was placed on her by my grandparents or great grandparents' actions? Remember, I said we are supernatural beings, and any "fix" would be supernatural also? It's incredibly simple, although not easy, five part puzzle.

The hardest part will be to see her problems as a spiritual issue. After that, it's a cakewalk!

Once she recognizes that it is a spiritual matter, she has to A) Confess that she has sin in her bloodline; and B) Repent for her own sin and the sin of her forefathers (including me and her natural father); by faith C) Believe that God wants to remove the curse and once she repents He immediately forgives her; and D) Receive the release from the curse. Again, use your Faith: Confess, Repent, Believe, Receive.

REPENTANCE is the KEY to a Curse-Free existence!

The easiest way to avoid generational curses is to not do anything wrong! However, since we are human, and our ancestors are human also, it is impossible to live a sin-free existence. What we can do is immediately repent for any sin that we do commit and receive immediate forgiveness, because otherwise unrepented sin becomes iniquity – the root of curses. God doesn't like iniquity! He loves repentance. He rewards them both equally, although differently...curses or blessings!

> *"He who covers his transgressions will not prosper, but whoever confesses and forsakes his sins will obtain mercy,"* (Proverbs 28:13).

CHAPTER EIGHT: WHEN DO I DO IT?

You are probably asking yourself IF and/or WHEN to actually cleanse your bloodline DNA. Here is a chart:

NO CHILDREN YET:

If you have no children yet, and you are saved, whether you did stupid stuff or not: Now would be the time to get rid of all generational curses, whether you are male or female! You can get all the curses off your bloodline AND the bloodline of your unborn children.

FUTURE SPOUSE:

Any future spouse that you marry will have to cleanse his or her generational bloodlines prior to the two of you actually becoming pregnant – because the curses are carried in your DNA. If you both fail to do it prior to getting pregnant, which is best and earliest, do it while the baby is in the womb. It will also work up to age 11 or so as long as the child lives in your home and you have authority over him or her, but obviously the younger the better. Don't you want your children to live curse-free? Do it now!

CHILDREN BEFORE SALVATION:

If you had children before you were saved, and you did stupid stuff, you can repent and cut the generational curses off both yourself and your children before they reach the age of accountability – again, as long as the child lives in your home and you have authority over him. The age of accountability is around 13-14 years old.

Once again, PLEASE do it as young as possible! We don't want children learning to smoke, or drink, or exploring their sexuality at a young age.

UNSAVED FAMILY:

If your parents were not saved before you had children, and you were not saved, then your children most certainly have generational curses on their lives. If they are still young, and living at home, you can repent and cleanse their bloodlines on their behalf AFTER you have cleansed your own.

However, if they are older and on their own, or living

with the other parent who is not saved...they must do it for themselves.

This is the hardest part—waiting for them to realize the hardships and heartaches they are going through have spiritual roots. They will also need to repent and cleanse their own bloodlines of any sin they have committed themselves before they pass the curses on to their own children.

CHAPTER NINE: THE OTHER SIDE

That brings us full circle. Jesus set me free, removing a huge boulder of a burden and I would like to do the same for you! He reminded me that the behaviors that I see operating in my children's lives are not my fault – literally!

Our children are not only subject to the generational curses from people they may not have even known on our side of the family - but also from the other parent's side.

See, I was lamenting to the Lord about all the issues my children seem to be having, feeling guilty about all that I did to contribute to their angst and their pain with my former iniquity and behavior patterns. The Lord interrupted me, and asked,

"Have you cleansed your bloodlines?"

Stunned, I said, "Yes, Lord. I have. Why is all this still happening, even though I have cleansed my bloodlines?"

Quietly, I heard Him respond, "Your children have

TWO PARENTS."

Immediately I felt a huge, heavy load lift off of me! See, I had already repented and cleansed our bloodlines on my side of their family tree, from my life backward...but the Lord reminded me that my children have two parents, so they have TWO SETS of bloodlines that need to be cleansed.

Neither of their fathers is saved; both are living in the world and not for Jesus. Neither one has cleansed their bloodlines of generational curses, so whatever curses were operating at the time my children were conceived are still In full force and effect until my children cleanse their own bloodlines at some future point in time ... which I am confident they will.

It is the same for your children. Once they have attained the age of accountability you can no longer speak for them. They will have to do it themselves. Even if you could, they have two parents, just like my children. Unless your child's other parent cleanses his/her bloodlines, your child will be under a curse, until your child does it for him or herself.

But the good news is this: once they cleanse their bloodlines and the bloodlines of their own children, they are cleansed – forever!

Jesus said,

> "You are cleansed and pruned already, because of the word which I have given you [the teachings I

have discussed with you]," (John 15:3 AMPC).

CHAPTER TEN: GENERATIONAL BLESSINGS

The One Thousand Generation Blessing!

And here's the best part: Now comes the blessings for One-Thousand generations!

> *"Know, recognize, and understand therefore that the Lord your God, He is God, the faithful God, Who keeps covenant and steadfast love and mercy with those who love Him and keep His commandments, to a thousand generations..."* (Deuteronomy 7:9 AMPC)

> *"But showing mercy and steadfast love to a thousand generations of those who love Me and keep My commandments,"* (Exodus 20:6 AMPC).

No more curses! Only blessings!

Thank God TODAY for showing you THE WAY!

Praise Jesus!

CHAPTER ELEVEN: DO NOT BE CONDEMNED

I hear the Lord saying,

The accuser of the brethren has been working overtime and My people are feeling condemned. This is not right.

> *Romans 8:1 "Therefore, [there is] now no condemnation (no adjudging guilty of wrong) for those who are in Christ Jesus, who live [and] walk not after the dictates of the flesh, but after the dictates of the Spirit."*

These are more than just words. Paul himself cried out to me on more than one occasion to remove the thorn from his flesh – his sin, his ungodly desires, those that he just couldn't stop doing!

> *"O unhappy and pitiable and wretched man that I am!" Romans 7:24*

> *"For I fail to practice the good deeds I desire to*

do, but the evil deeds that I do not desire to do are what I am ever doing." Romans 7:19

My people believe that because they carry My Spirit that they are to be perfect – they should not do or think the evil ways that they do. I am here to say that is simply not truth. You are becoming perfected...you don't start out that way!

Understand that there is much more going on in the spiritual world that filters into your natural world than you will ever know or understand. In fact, it would take all eternity to figure it out. All of it impacts your thought life, your actionable life and your spiritual life...even your prayer life.

I know these things and I do not fault you, and here is proof, for my friend Paul experienced and wrote about what I want you to KNOW in your heart:

"14 We know that the Law is spiritual; but I am a creature of the flesh [carnal, unspiritual], having been sold into slavery under [the control of] sin.

15 For I do not understand my own actions [I am baffled, bewildered]. I do not practice or accomplish what I wish, but I do the very thing that I loathe [which my moral instinct condemns].

16 Now if I do [habitually] what is contrary to my

desire, [that means that] I acknowledge and agree that the Law is good (morally excellent) and that I take sides with it.

17 However, it is no longer I who do the deed, but the sin [principle] which is at home in me and has possession of me.

18 For I know that nothing good dwells within me, that is, in my flesh. I can will what is right, but I cannot perform it. [I have the intention and urge to do what is right, but no power to carry it out.]

19 For I fail to practice the good deeds I desire to do, but the evil deeds that I do not desire to do are what I am [ever] doing.

20 Now if I do what I do not desire to do, it is no longer I doing it [it is not myself that acts], but the sin [principle] which dwells within me [fixed and operating in my soul].

21 So I find it to be a law (rule of action of my being) that when I want to do what is right and good, evil is ever present with me and I am subject to its insistent demands.

22 For I endorse and delight in the Law of God in my inmost self [with my new nature]. [Ps. 1:2.]

23 But I discern in my bodily members [in the

sensitive appetites and wills of the flesh] a different law (rule of action) at war against the law of my mind (my reason) and making me a prisoner to the law of sin that dwells in my bodily organs [in the sensitive appetites and wills of the flesh]."

Romans 7:14-23

And here is how you are judged this day:

> *"Straightening up, Jesus said to her, "Woman, where are they? Did no one condemn you?"*
>
> *She answered, "No one, Lord!" And Jesus said, "I do not condemn you either. Go. From now on sin no more." (John 8:10-11)*

Before I came to earth you would have been stoned for your sins. But since I have come - *and am still here now* - I forgive you, even before you become perfected!

I say to you today, "Go and Sin No More." I know you cannot be perfect, and I do not expect that. One day you shall be, when you sit with me in my temple in heaven. Then, sin will have no more rule or reign over you, because you will have no more earthly bodily members (see Romans 7:23 above).

Until then, know I love you! There has never been a moment when you were unloved – even

AS you were sinning, I still loved you, and I ever shall. You are mine. You are branded. You are my child and I will NEVER change my mind about you.

Prophetic Word given to Edie Bayer

ABOUT THE AUTHOR: EDIE BAYER

Edie Bayer is a prophetic voice to the nations. She and her husband, Darryl Bayer, together minister through Kingdom Promoters Ministry (http://www.KingdomPromoters.org). As an Apostle, she set into order a new fellowship network initiative: "Get Connected", a branch of "God's Family Network". God is reordering His church to look like the early church again. God's Family Network endeavors to connect small groups of brethren in home based family networks to fellowship, worship, break bread and live life together. You can find God's Family Network at www.GodsFamilyNetwork.com . She travels, preaches, writes, prophesies and mentors up-and-coming prophets and apostles. Edie's prophetic words can be found on Elijah List, Global Prophetic Voice, Women of Impact among many other online newsletters. Edie has eight books, which can be found at Kingdom Promoters' website as well as Amazon.com. Edie also helps authors get their books into print. Visit www.GlorifiedPublishing.com for more information

www.ingramcontent.com/pod-product-compliance
Lightning Source LLC
Chambersburg PA
CBHW071939020426
42331CB00010B/2940